QUILTER'S 2020
PLANNER

Belongs To:

_____

_____

Halloween horror – when someone discovers your fabric stash!

SEPTEMBER
M T W T F S S
              1
2 3 4 5 6 7 8
9 10 11 12 13 14 15
16 17 18 19 20 21 22
23 24 25 26 27 28 29
30

OCTOBER 2019

NOVEMBER
M T W T F S S
          1 2 3
4 5 6 7 8 9 10
11 12 13 14 15 16 17
18 19 20 21 22 23 24
25 26 27 28 29 30

Mon	Tue	Wed	Thu	Fri	Sat	Sun
30	1	2	3	4	5	6
7	8	9	10	11	12	13
14 Columbus Day	15	16	17	18	19	20
21	22	23	24	25	26	27
28	29	30	31 Halloween	1	2	3

Week of _____

Monday		√	To Do
Tuesday			
Wednesday			
Thursday			
Friday			
Saturday			
Sunday			

Week of _____

Monday		✓	*To Do*
Tuesday			
Wednesday			
Thursday			
Friday			
Saturday			
Sunday			

Week of _____

Monday	√	*To Do*
Tuesday		
Wednesday		
Thursday		
Friday		
Saturday		
Sunday		

Week of _____

Monday		√	To Do
Tuesday			
Wednesday			
Thursday			
Friday			
Saturday			
Sunday			

Week of _____

	Monday
	Tuesday
	Wednesday
	Thursday
	Friday
	Saturday
	Sunday

√	To Do

Quilters Never Grow Old, They Just Fall To Pieces.

NOVEMBER 2019

OCTOBER
M T W T F S S
1 2 3 4 5 6
7 8 9 10 11 12 13
14 15 16 17 18 19 20
21 22 23 24 25 26 27
28 29 30 31

DECEMBER
M T W T F S S
1
2 3 4 5 6 7 8
9 10 11 12 13 14 15
16 17 18 19 20 21 22
23 24 25 26 27 28 29
30 31

Mon	Tue	Wed	Thu	Fri	Sat	Sun
28	29	30	31	1 All Saints Day	2	3 Daylight Savings Time Ends
4	5	6	7	8	9	10
11 Veteran's Day	12	13	14	15	16	17
18	19	20	21	22	23	24
25	26	27	28 Thanksgiving Day	29	30	

Week of _____

	Monday
	Tuesday
	Wednesday
	Thursday
	Friday
	Saturday
	Sunday

√	To Do

Week of _____

Monday

Tuesday

Wednesday

Thursday

Friday

Saturday

Sunday

√	To Do

Week of _____

Monday		√	To Do
Tuesday			
Wednesday			
Thursday			
Friday			
Saturday			
Sunday			

Week of _____

Day	
Monday	
Tuesday	
Wednesday	
Thursday	
Friday	
Saturday	
Sunday	

√	To Do

Week of _____

Monday		
Tuesday		
Wednesday		
Thursday		
Friday		
Saturday		
Sunday		

√	To Do

A hand-made quilt is the best gift of all.

DECEMBER 2019

NOVEMBER

M	T	W	T	F	S	S
				1	2	3
4	5	6	7	8	9	10
11	12	13	14	15	16	17
18	19	20	21	22	23	24
25	26	27	28	29	30	

JANUARY 2020

M	T	W	T	F	S	S
		1	2	3	4	5
6	7	8	9	10	11	12
13	14	15	16	17	18	19
20	21	22	23	24	25	26
27	28	29	30	31		

Mon	Tue	Wed	Thu	Fri	Sat	Sun
25	26	27	28	29	30	1 First Sunday of Advent
2	3	4	5	6	7 Pearl Harbor Remembrance Day	8
9	10	11	12	13	14	15
16	17	18	19	20	21	22 First Day of Winter
23	24 Christmas Eve	25 Christmas	26	27	28	29
30	31 New Year's Eve	1	2	3	4	5

Week of _____

Monday

Tuesday

Wednesday

Thursday

Friday

Saturday

Sunday

√	To Do

Week of _____

Day	
Monday	
Tuesday	
Wednesday	
Thursday	
Friday	
Saturday	
Sunday	

✓	To Do

Week of _____

Monday		√	To Do
Tuesday			
Wednesday			
Thursday			
Friday			
Saturday			
Sunday			

Week of _____

	Monday

	Tuesday

	Wednesday

	Thursday

	Friday

	Saturday

	Sunday

√	To Do

Week of _____

Monday		√	To Do
Tuesday			
Wednesday			
Thursday			
Friday			
Saturday			
Sunday			

I quilt so I don't kill people.

JANUARY 2020

December 2019
M T W T F S S
                1
2 3 4 5 6 7 8
9 10 11 12 13 14 15
16 17 18 19 20 21 22
23 24 25 26 27 28 29
30 31

February
M T W T F S S
          1 2
3 4 5 6 7 8 9
10 11 12 13 14 15 16
17 18 19 20 21 22 23
24 25 26 27 28 29

Mon	Tue	Wed	Thu	Fri	Sat	Sun
30	31	1 New Year's Day	2	3	4	5
6 Epiphany	7	8	9	10	11	12
13	14	15	16	17	18	19
20 Martin Luther King Jr.'s Birthday	21	22	23	24	25	26
27	28	29	30	31	1	2

Week of _____

Monday		√	*To Do*
Tuesday			
Wednesday			
Thursday			
Friday			
Saturday			
Sunday			

Week of _____

	√	To Do
Monday		
Tuesday		
Wednesday		
Thursday		
Friday		
Saturday		
Sunday		

Week of _____

Monday		
Tuesday		
Wednesday		
Thursday		
Friday		
Saturday		
Sunday		

√	To Do

Week of _____

Monday		√	To Do
Tuesday			
Wednesday			
Thursday			
Friday			
Saturday			
Sunday			

Week of _____

Monday		√	To Do
Tuesday			
Wednesday			
Thursday			
Friday			
Saturday			
Sunday			

I only quilt on days that end in 'Y'.

FEBRUARY 2020

JANUARY
M T W T F S S
        1 2 3 4 5
6 7 8 9 10 11 12
13 14 15 16 17 18 19
20 21 22 23 24 25 26
27 28 29 30 31

MARCH
M T W T F S S
                 1
2 3 4 5 6 7 8
9 10 11 12 13 14 15
16 17 18 19 20 21 22
23 24 25 26 27 28 29
30 31

Mon	Tue	Wed	Thu	Fri	Sat	Sun
27	28	29	30	31	1	2 Groundhog Day
3	4	5	6	7	8	9
10	11	12 Lincoln's Birthday	13	14 Valentine's Day	15	16
17 President's Day	18	19	20	21	22 Washington's Birthday	23
24 Mardi Gras	25	26 Ash Wednesday	27	28	29	1

Week of _____

Monday		√	To Do
Tuesday			
Wednesday			
Thursday			
Friday			
Saturday			
Sunday			

Week of _____

Monday		√	To Do
Tuesday			
Wednesday			
Thursday			
Friday			
Saturday			
Sunday			

Week of _____

Monday		√	To Do
Tuesday			
Wednesday			
Thursday			
Friday			
Saturday			
Sunday			

Week of _____

Monday		√	To Do
Tuesday			
Wednesday			
Thursday			
Friday			
Saturday			
Sunday			

Week of _____

	Monday

	Tuesday

	Wednesday

	Thursday

	Friday

	Saturday

	Sunday

√	To Do

Keep calm, and grab the seam ripper.

MARCH 2020

FEBRUARY
M T W T F S S
              1 2
3 4 5 6 7 8 9
10 11 12 13 14 15 16
17 18 19 20 21 22 23
24 25 26 27 28 29

APRIL
M T W T F S S
        1 2 3 4 5
6 7 8 9 10 11 12
13 14 15 16 17 18 19
20 21 22 23 24 25 26
27 28 29 30

Mon	Tue	Wed	Thu	Fri	Sat	Sun
24	25	26	27	28	29	1
2	3	4	5	6	7	8
9	10	11	12	13	14	15
16	17 St. Patrick's Day	18	19	20 First Day of Spring	21	22
23	24	25	26	27	28	29
30	31	1	2	3	4	5

Week of _____

Monday		✓	To Do
Tuesday			
Wednesday			
Thursday			
Friday			
Saturday			
Sunday			

Week of _____

	Monday

	Tuesday

	Wednesday

	Thursday

	Friday

	Saturday

	Sunday

√	To Do

Week of _____

Monday		√	To Do
Tuesday			
Wednesday			
Thursday			
Friday			
Saturday			
Sunday			

Week of _____

Monday		√	To Do

	√	To Do
Monday		
Tuesday		
Wednesday		
Thursday		
Friday		
Saturday		
Sunday		

Week of _____

	Monday

Tuesday

Wednesday

Thursday

Friday

Saturday

Sunday

√	To Do

Thank goodness for my fat quarters!

APRIL 2020

March

M	T	W	T	F	S	S
						1
2	3	4	5	6	7	8
9	10	11	12	13	14	15
16	17	18	19	20	21	22
23	24	25	26	27	28	29
30	31					

May

M	T	W	T	F	S	S
				1	2	3
4	5	6	7	8	9	10
11	12	13	14	15	16	17
18	19	20	21	22	23	24
25	26	27	28	29	30	31

Mon	Tue	Wed	Thu	Fri	Sat	Sun
30	31	1 April Fool's Day	2	3	4	5 Palm Sunday
6	7	8	9 Maundy Thursday	10 Good Friday	11 Holy Saturday	12 Easter
13	14	15	16	17	18	19
20	21	22	23	24	25	26
27	28	29	30	1	2	3

Week of _____

Monday		√	To Do
Tuesday			
Wednesday			
Thursday			
Friday			
Saturday			
Sunday			

Week of _____

Day	
Monday	
Tuesday	
Wednesday	
Thursday	
Friday	
Saturday	
Sunday	

√	To Do

Week of _____

Monday		√	To Do
Tuesday			
Wednesday			
Thursday			
Friday			
Saturday			
Sunday			

Week of _____

Day	
Monday	
Tuesday	
Wednesday	
Thursday	
Friday	
Saturday	
Sunday	

√	To Do

Week of _____

	Monday

	Tuesday

	Wednesday

	Thursday

	Friday

	Saturday

	Sunday

√	To Do

Quilters know all the angles.

MAY 2020

April
M T W T F S S
         1 2 3 4 5
6 7 8 9 10 11 12
13 14 15 16 17 18 19
20 21 22 23 24 25 26
27 28 29 30

June
M T W T F S S
         1 2 3 4 5 6 7
8 9 10 11 12 13 14
15 16 17 18 19 20 21
22 23 24 25 26 27 28
29 30

Mon	Tue	Wed	Thu	Fri	Sat	Sun
27	28	29	30	1	2	3
4	5 Cinco De Mayo	6	7 National Day of Prayer	8	9	10 Mother's Day
11	12	13	14	15	16	17
18	19	20	21 Ascension Day	22	23	24
25 Memorial Day	26	27	28	29	30	31 Pentecost

Week of _____

Monday		√	To Do
Tuesday			
Wednesday			
Thursday			
Friday			
Saturday			
Sunday			

Week of _____

	√	To Do
Monday		
Tuesday		
Wednesday		
Thursday		
Friday		
Saturday		
Sunday		

Week of _____

Monday		√	To Do
Tuesday			
Wednesday			
Thursday			
Friday			
Saturday			
Sunday			

Week of _____

Day		√	To Do
Monday			
Tuesday			
Wednesday			
Thursday			
Friday			
Saturday			
Sunday			

Week of _____

Monday		√	To Do
Tuesday			
Wednesday			
Thursday			
Friday			
Saturday			
Sunday			

The one who dies with the most fabric wins.

JUNE 2020

May
M T W T F S S
          1 2 3
4 5 6 7 8 9 10
11 12 13 14 15 16 17
18 19 20 21 22 23 24
25 26 27 28 29 30 31

July
M T W T F S S
      1 2 3 4 5
6 7 8 9 10 11 12
13 14 15 16 17 18 19
20 21 22 23 24 25 26
27 28 29 30 31

Mon	Tue	Wed	Thu	Fri	Sat	Sun
1	2	3	4	5	6	7
8	9	10	11	12	13	14
15	16	17	18	19	20 First Day of Summer	21 Father's Day
22	23	24	25	26	27	28
29	30	1	2	3	4	5

Week of _____

Monday		√	To Do
Tuesday			
Wednesday			
Thursday			
Friday			
Saturday			
Sunday			

Week of _____

	Monday
	Tuesday
	Wednesday
	Thursday
	Friday
	Saturday
	Sunday

√	To Do

Week of _____

Day	
Monday	
Tuesday	
Wednesday	
Thursday	
Friday	
Saturday	
Sunday	

√	To Do

Week of _____

	Monday

	Tuesday

	Wednesday

	Thursday

	Friday

	Saturday

	Sunday

√	To Do

Week of _____

Day	
Monday	
Tuesday	
Wednesday	
Thursday	
Friday	
Saturday	
Sunday	

✓	To Do

Quilting warms the heart and feeds the soul.

JULY 2020

JUNE
M T W T F S S
1 2 3 4 5 6 7
8 9 10 11 12 13 14
15 16 17 18 19 20 21
22 23 24 25 26 27 28
29 30

AUGUST
M T W T F S S
1 2
3 4 5 6 7 8 9
10 11 12 13 14 15 16
17 18 19 20 21 22 23
24 25 26 27 28 29 30
31

Mon	Tue	Wed	Thu	Fri	Sat	Sun
29	30	1	2	3	4 Independence Day	5
6	7	8	9	10	11	12
13	14	15	16	17	18	19
20	21	22	23	24	25	26
27	28	29	30	31	1	2

Week of _____

	Monday

	Tuesday

	Wednesday

	Thursday

	Friday

	Saturday

	Sunday

√	To Do

Week of _____

	Monday

	Tuesday

	Wednesday

	Thursday

	Friday

	Saturday

	Sunday

√	To Do

Week of _____

Monday		√	To Do
Tuesday			
Wednesday			
Thursday			
Friday			
Saturday			
Sunday			

Week of _____

Monday		√	To Do
Tuesday			
Wednesday			
Thursday			
Friday			
Saturday			
Sunday			

Week of _____

Monday		√	To Do
Tuesday			
Wednesday			
Thursday			
Friday			
Saturday			
Sunday			

Anytime is a great time for quilting.

AUGUST 2020

July
M T W T F S S
          1 2 3 4 5
6 7 8 9 10 11 12
13 14 15 16 17 18 19
20 21 22 23 24 25 26
27 28 29 30 31

September
M T W T F S S
             1 2 3 4 5 6
7 8 9 10 11 12 13
14 15 16 17 18 19 20
21 22 23 24 25 26 27
28 29 30

Mon	Tue	Wed	Thu	Fri	Sat	Sun
27	28	29	30	31	1	2
3	4	5	6	7	8	9
10	11	12	13	14	15	16
17	18	19	20	21	22	23
24	25	26	27	28	29	30
31	1	2	3	4	5	6

Week of _____

Monday		√	To Do
Tuesday			
Wednesday			
Thursday			
Friday			
Saturday			
Sunday			

Week of _____

Monday		√	To Do
Tuesday			
Wednesday			
Thursday			
Friday			
Saturday			
Sunday			

Week of _____

Monday		√	To Do
Tuesday			
Wednesday			
Thursday			
Friday			
Saturday			
Sunday			

Week of _____

Monday		√	To Do
Tuesday			
Wednesday			
Thursday			
Friday			
Saturday			
Sunday			

Week of _____

Monday		√	To Do
Tuesday			
Wednesday			
Thursday			
Friday			
Saturday			
Sunday			

Eat, sleep, quilt, repeat...

SEPTEMBER 2020

August
M T W T F S S
                1 2
3 4 5 6 7 8 9
10 11 12 13 14 15 16
17 18 19 20 21 22 23
24 25 26 27 28 29 30
31

October
M T W T F S S
                1 2 3 4
5 6 7 8 9 10 11
12 13 14 15 16 17 18
19 20 21 22 23 24 25
26 27 28 29 30 31

Mon	Tue	Wed	Thu	Fri	Sat	Sun
31	1	2	3	4	5	6
7 Labor Day	8	9	10	11 Patriot Day	12	13
14	15	16	17	18	19	20
21	22 First Day of Autumn	23	24	25	26	27
28	29	30	1	2	3	4

Week of _____

Monday

Tuesday

Wednesday

Thursday

Friday

Saturday

Sunday

√	To Do

Week of _____

Monday		√	To Do
Tuesday			
Wednesday			
Thursday			
Friday			
Saturday			
Sunday			

Week of _____

	Monday

√	To Do

Tuesday

Wednesday

Thursday

Friday

Saturday

Sunday

Week of _____

| | Monday |
| | |

| | Tuesday |
| | |

| | Wednesday |
| | |

| | Thursday |
| | |

| | Friday |
| | |

| | Saturday |
| | |

| | Sunday |
| | |

√	To Do

Week of _____

Monday		√	To Do
Tuesday			
Wednesday			
Thursday			
Friday			
Saturday			
Sunday			

Quilters love material wealth.

OCTOBER 2020

September
M T W T F S S
1 2 3 4 5 6
7 8 9 10 11 12 13
14 15 16 17 18 19 20
21 22 23 24 25 26 27
28 29 30

November
M T W T F S S
1
2 3 4 5 6 7 8
9 10 11 12 13 14 15
16 17 18 19 20 21 22
23 24 25 26 27 28 29
30

Mon	Tue	Wed	Thu	Fri	Sat	Sun
28	29	30	1	2	3	4
5	6	7	8	9	10	11
12 Columbus Day	13	14	15	16	17	18
19	20	21	22	23	24	25
26	27	28	29	30	31 Halloween	1

Week of _____

	Monday

	Tuesday

	Wednesday

	Thursday

	Friday

	Saturday

	Sunday

√	To Do

Week of _____

Monday

Tuesday

Wednesday

Thursday

Friday

Saturday

Sunday

√	To Do

Week of _____

Monday		√	To Do
Tuesday			
Wednesday			
Thursday			
Friday			
Saturday			
Sunday			

Week of _____

Monday		√	To Do

	√	To Do
Monday		
Tuesday		
Wednesday		
Thursday		
Friday		
Saturday		
Sunday		

Week of _____

Monday		✔	To Do
Tuesday			
Wednesday			
Thursday			
Friday			
Saturday			
Sunday			

Quilt now, sleep later.

November 2020

October
M T W T F S S
          1 2 3 4
5 6 7 8 9 10 11
12 13 14 15 16 17 18
19 20 21 22 23 24 25
26 27 28 29 30 31

December
M T W T F S S
    1 2 3 4 5 6
7 8 9 10 11 12 13
14 15 16 17 18 19 20
21 22 23 24 25 26 27
28 29 30 31

Mon	Tue	Wed	Thu	Fri	Sat	Sun
26	27	28	29	30	31	1 All Saints Day Daylight Savings Time Ends
2	3 Election Day	4	5	6	7	8
9	10	11 Veteran's Day	12	13	14	15
16	17	18	19	20	21	22
23	24	25	26 Thanksgiving Day	27	28	29 First Sunday of Advent
30	1	2	3	4	5	6

Week of _____

| | Monday |
| | |

| | Tuesday |
| | |

| | Wednesday |
| | |

| | Thursday |
| | |

| | Friday |
| | |

| | Saturday |
| | |

| | Sunday |
| | |

√	To Do

Week of _____

	Monday
	Tuesday
	Wednesday
	Thursday
	Friday
	Saturday
	Sunday

√	To Do

Week of _____

Monday		√	To Do
Tuesday			
Wednesday			
Thursday			
Friday			
Saturday			
Sunday			

Week of _____

Day	
Monday	
Tuesday	
Wednesday	
Thursday	
Friday	
Saturday	
Sunday	

√	To Do

Week of _____

Monday		√	To Do
Tuesday			
Wednesday			
Thursday			
Friday			
Saturday			
Sunday			

I don't want to look back and think, 'I wish I had bought that fabric'.

DECEMBER 2020

November
M T W T F S S
30 1
2 3 4 5 6 7 8
9 10 11 12 13 14 15
16 17 18 19 20 21 22
23 24 25 26 27 28 29
30

January 2021
M T W T F S S
1 2 3
4 5 6 7 8 9 10
11 12 13 14 15 16 17
18 19 20 21 22 23 24
25 26 27 28 29 30 31

Mon	Tue	Wed	Thu	Fri	Sat	Sun
30	1	2	3	4	5	6
7 Pearl Harbor Remembrance Day	8	9	10	11	12	13
14	15	16	17	18	19	20
21 First Day of Winter	22	23	24 Christmas Eve	25 Christmas	26	27
28	29	30	31 New Year's Eve	1	2	3

Week of _____

Monday		√	To Do
Tuesday			
Wednesday			
Thursday			
Friday			
Saturday			
Sunday			

Week of _____

Monday			To Do
	√		
Tuesday			
Wednesday			
Thursday			
Friday			
Saturday			
Sunday			

Week of _____

Monday		√	To Do
Tuesday			
Wednesday			
Thursday			
Friday			
Saturday			
Sunday			

Week of _____

Monday		

	√	To Do
Tuesday		
Wednesday		
Thursday		
Friday		
Saturday		
Sunday		

Week of _____

	Monday

	Tuesday

	Wednesday

	Thursday

	Friday

	Saturday

	Sunday

√	To Do

Notes:

Quilt Sizes

BABY QUILT	36" X 54"
TWIN QUILT	54" X 90"
FULL QUILT	72" X 90"
QUEEN QUILT	90" X 108"
KING QUILT	108" X 108"

Mattress Sizes

BABY QUILT	27" X 50"
TWIN QUILT	39" X 75"
FULL QUILT	54" X 75"
QUEEN QUILT	60" X 80"
KING QUILT	72" X 84"

Yards to Inches

1/8 YARD	4.5 INCHES
1/4 YARD	9 INCHES
1/3 YARD	12 INCHES
3/8 YARD	13.5 INCHES
1/2 YARD	18 INCHES
5/8 YARD	22.5 INCHES
2/3 YARD	24 INCHES
3/4 YARD	27 INCHES
7/8 YARD	31.5 INCHES
1 YARD	36 INCHES

Notes

Notes

Notes

Notes

Notes

Notes

Notes

Notes

Notes

Notes

Notes

Notes

Notes

Notes

Notes